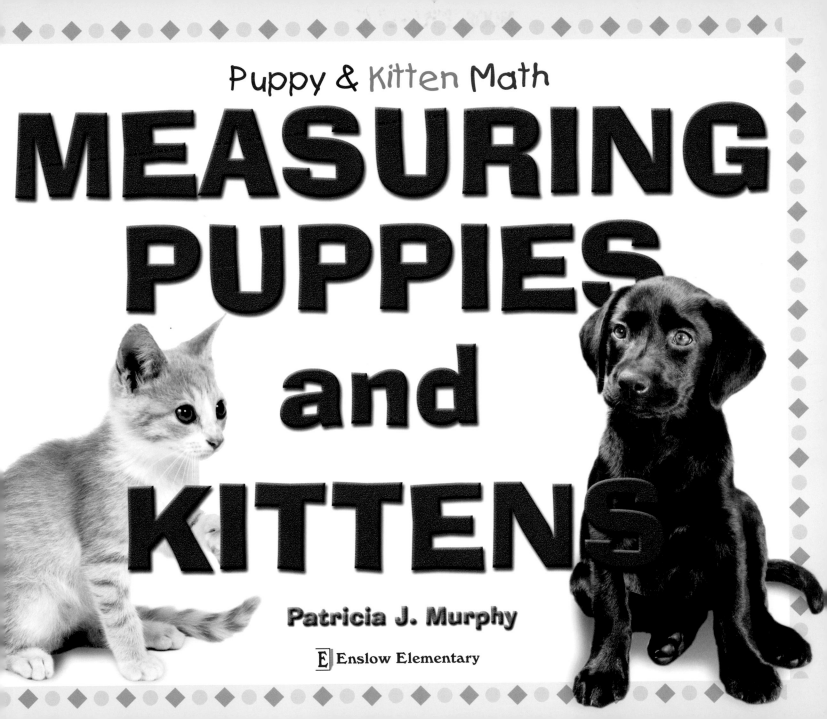

Puppy & Kitten Math

MEASURING PUPPIES and KITTENS

Patricia J. Murphy

Enslow Elementary

Contents

Words to Know

height—A measure of how high something is.

inch—A unit of measurement. There are 12 inches in a foot and 36 inches in a yard.

length—A measure of how long something is.

measure—To find the size, weight, or amount of something.

measurement—The size of something.

width—A measure of how wide something is.

Measuring Things

We **measure** to find out the size of something. When we measure things, we get their **measurements**. Measurements tell us how big or small something is.

BIG!

small!

Without measurements,

- ✔ we would not know how tall we are.
- ✔ we could not cook our favorite recipes the same every time.
- ✔ we could not make most things like houses, cars, clothes, or toys. Yikes!

Turn the page and start measuring puppies and kittens.

Nonstandard Measurements

Let's measure Pal.

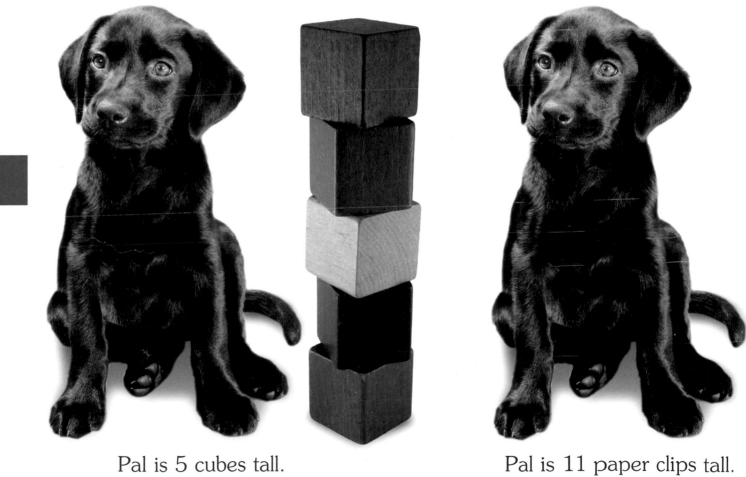

Pal is 5 cubes tall.

Pal is 11 paper clips tall.

Pal's measurements are different. Do you know why? Cubes, paper clips, and hands are different sizes.

How can his measurements be the same? Turn the page to find out.

Pal is 3 hands tall.

Long ago, people used their bodies to measure things. They used their hands, fingers, or the distance from their elbows to second fingers.

Standard Measurements

Let's measure Pal again.

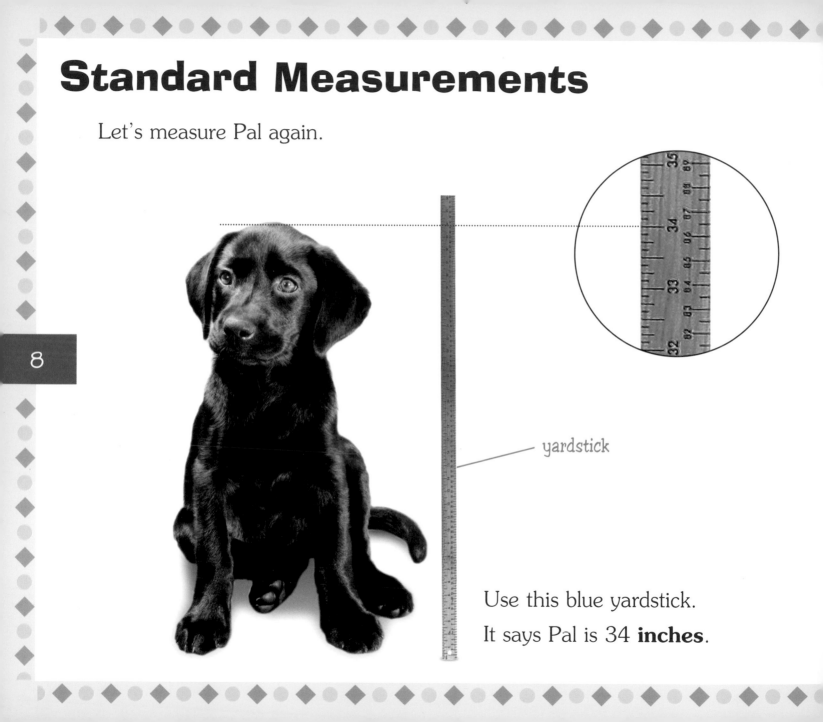

yardstick

Use this blue yardstick.

It says Pal is 34 **inches**.

Use this yellow yardstick.
It says Pal is 34 inches, too.

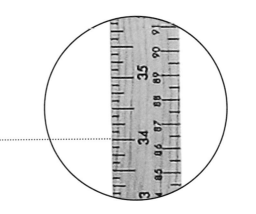

Both yardsticks used the same unit
of measurement—the inch.
Their measurements are the same.
Hurray!

In the United States, we use
the inch for measuring how long,
tall, or wide something is.
1 foot = 12 inches
1 yard = 36 inches

How to Measure

Here are a few tips to use when measuring:

1. Place your ruler or other measuring tool next to the object you are measuring.

2. Line up one end of the object with the end of your ruler. Remember to start at zero.

You have found your measurement. This kitten is 11 inches tall.

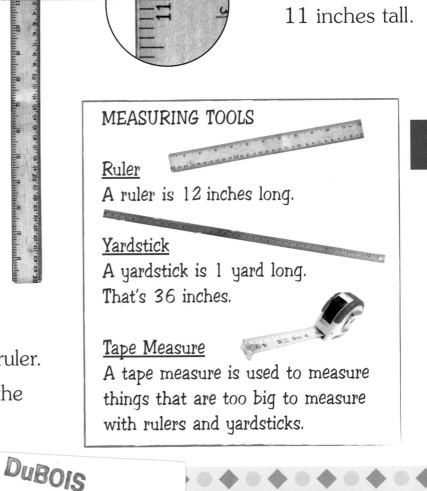

MEASURING TOOLS

Ruler
A ruler is 12 inches long.

Yardstick
A yardstick is 1 yard long. That's 36 inches.

Tape Measure
A tape measure is used to measure things that are too big to measure with rulers and yardsticks.

3. Look at the other end of the ruler. What number does it read at the other end of your object?

Measuring Height

Puppies and kittens can be different **heights**. Height is how tall or how high something is. Let's measure how tall Max and Sam are.

Max's height is 17 inches.

Always measure things *twice*. It is a good way to make sure your measurement is right.

13

Sam's height is 18 inches.

How High Is the Doghouse Door?

Some puppies sleep in doghouses. Let's measure Tuffy's doghouse.

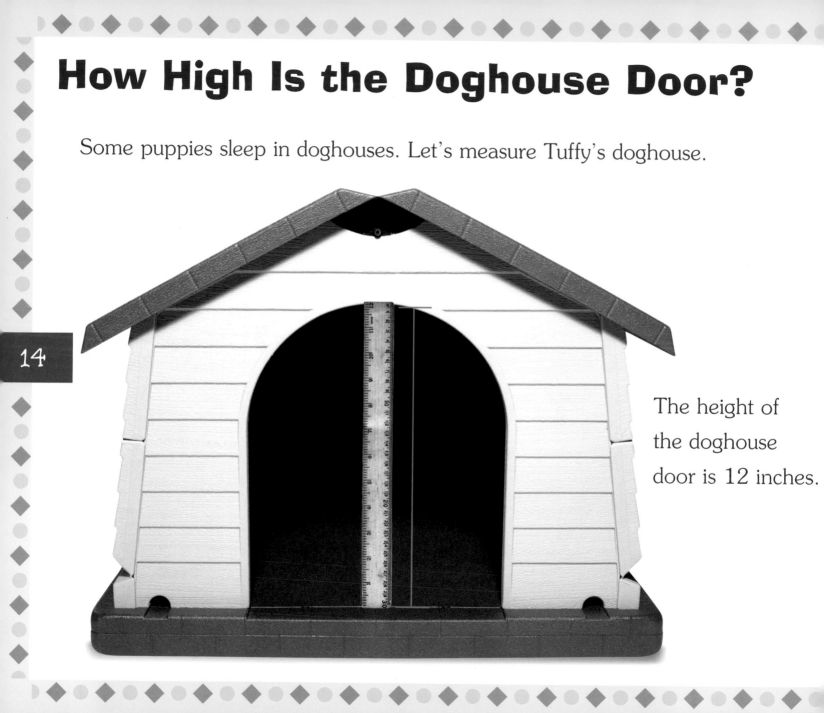

The height of the doghouse door is 12 inches.

How tall is Tuffy?

15

Always label, or write down, your measurements with the unit of measurement you are using. Tuffy's height is 16 **inches**.

Tuffy's height is 16 inches.

16 inches is more than 12 inches. Tuffy will have to bend down to get into his doghouse.

Watch your head, Tuffy!

How High Do They Jump?

Kittens like to jump on things!
How high did Muffin jump?
How high did Rocky jump?

Muffin jumped 6 inches high.

Rocky jumped 9 inches high.

Which kitten jumped higher?

17

Measuring Length

Length is how long something is. It is the distance from one end of something to the other. Let's measure the length of these tails.

Lucy's tail is 5 inches long.

Rex's tail is 3 inches long.

Which tail is the longest?

Which tail is the shortest?

Tabby's tail is 4 inches long.

Gabby's tail is 7 inches long.

How Long Are Their Bodies?

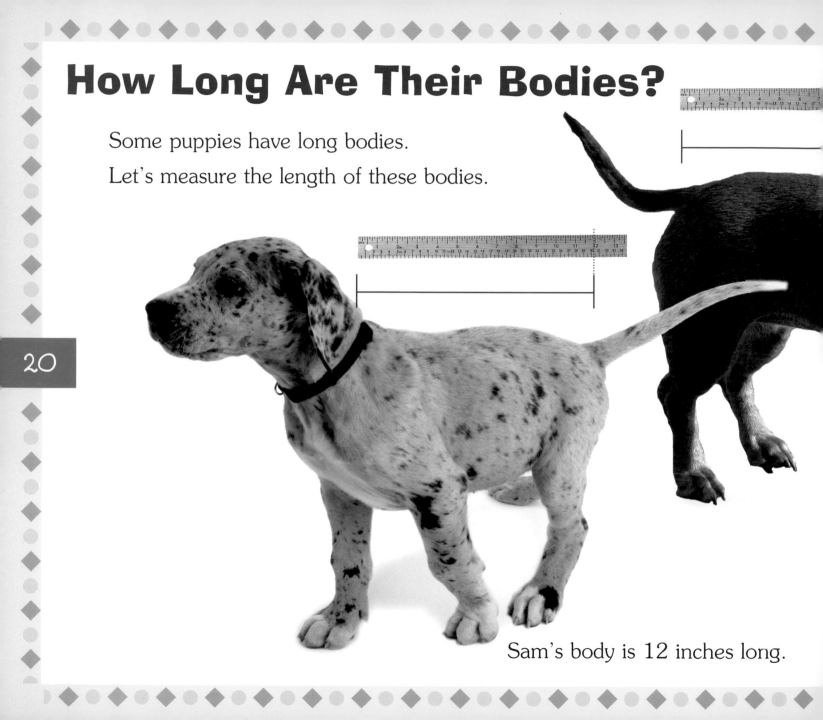

Some puppies have long bodies.

Let's measure the length of these bodies.

Sam's body is 12 inches long.

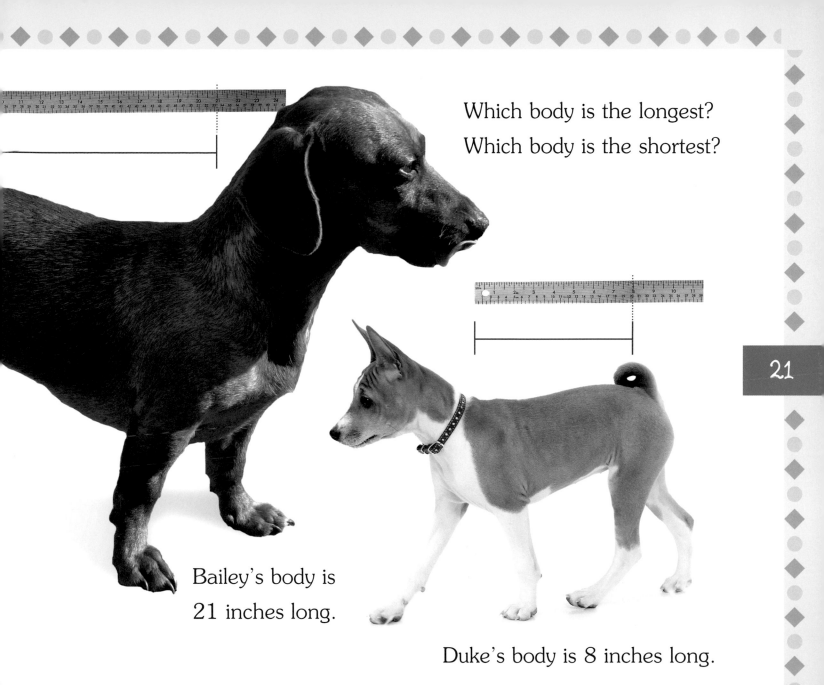

Which body is the longest?
Which body is the shortest?

Bailey's body is
21 inches long.

Duke's body is 8 inches long.

How Long Is the Yarn?

All kittens play with yarn!

Measure these pieces of yarn.

Kit's yarn is 6 inches long.

Mimi's and Pixie's yarn is 17 inches long.

Which yarn is the shortest?
Which is the longest?

Coco's yarn is 8 inches long.

Jada's yarn is
14 inches long.

Measuring Width

Width is how wide something is. It is the distance from one side of something to the other side. Let's measure the widths of Jack's, Max's, and Buddy's paws!

Which paw is the widest?

Jack's paw is 5 inches wide.

Max's paw is 3 inches wide.

Buddy's paw is 2 inches wide.

How Wide Are Their Heads?

How wide is Molly's head?

How wide is Jade's head?

Molly's head is 9 inches wide.

Jade's head is 8 inches wide.

Which head is the widest?

How Wide Are Their Bodies?

Fluffy and Buttons never stop eating.

Their bodies are growing wide.

How wide are their bodies?

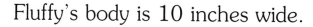

Fluffy's body is 10 inches wide.

Which body is the widest?

Buttons' body is
16 inches wide.

Ways to Keep Measuring

Keep Measuring

Measure your own puppies and kittens and write their measurements in a book. Keep track of how tall, wide, and long they grow. Try using inches and centimeters.

Measure Yourself

Have someone trace your body on a big piece of paper. Measure the length and width of your head, nose, ears, arms, hands, fingers, hips, legs, feet, and toes.

Make a Good Guess

Make a guess about the size of something before you measure it. Then compare your guess to the actual measurement. The more you guess, the closer your guesses will get!

Learn More

Books

Adler, David A. *How Tall, How Short, How Faraway*. New York: Holiday House, 1999.

Pistoia, Sara. *Measurement*. Chanhassen, Minn.: Child's World, 2003.

Schwartz, David. *Millions to Measure*. New York: Harper Collins, 2003.

Scott, Janine. *Why We Measure*. Mankato, Minn.: Compass Point Books, 2003.

Web Sites

The World of Measurement
http://oncampus.richmond.edu/
    academics/education/projects/
    webunits/measurement/

AAA Math: Measurements
http://www.aaamath.com/mea.html

Index

Series Math Consultant
Eileen Fernández, Ph.D.
Associate Professor, Mathematics Education
Montclair State University
Montclair, NJ

Series Literacy Consultant
Allan A. De Fina, Ph.D.
Past President of the New Jersey Reading Association
Professor, Department of Literacy Education
New Jersey City University
Jersey City, NJ

To my doggone great family—my love for you is without measure.

Acknowledgments: The author thanks Arlington Heights School District #25, in Arlington Heights, IL, and Lake Forest School District #67, in Lake Forest, IL, for their assistance in the research of this book.

Enslow Elementary, an imprint of Enslow Publishers, Inc.
Enslow Elementary® is a registered trademark of
Enslow Publishers, Inc.

Library of Congress Cataloging-in-Publication Data

Murphy, Patricia J., 1963–
 Measuring puppies and kittens / by Patricia J. Murphy.
  p. cm. — (Puppy and kitten math)
 Includes bibliographical references and index.
 ISBN-13: 978-0-7660-2727-5
 ISBN-10: 0-7660-2727-9
 1. Mensuration—Juvenile literature. 2. Weights and measures—Juvenile literature. I. Title.
 QA465.M84 2007
 516'.15—dc22
                                    2006004835

Printed in the United States of America

10 9 8 7 6 5 4 3 2 1

To Our Readers: We have done our best to make sure all Internet Addresses in this book were active and appropriate when we went to press. However, the author and the publisher have no control over and assume no liability for the material available on those Internet sites or on other Web sites they may link to. Any comments or suggestions can be sent by e-mail to comments@enslow.com or to the address on the back cover.

Photo credits: © Animal Attitude Brand X, p. 27; © Hemera Technologies, p. 5 cooking tools; © iStockphoto/Amanda Rohde, p. 26; © iStockphoto/ Henri Caroline, p. 23 Coco; © iStockphoto.com/Justin Horrocks, pp. 1 puppy, 6–9, 18 bull dog pup; © iStockphoto/Tony Campbell, p. 22 two kittens with yarn; © Jane Burton/Photo Researchers, Inc., pp. 1 kitten, 19 red tabby kitten, 28; © 2006 Jupiterimages Corporation, p. 8 yardstick, 15; © 2001 PhotoDisc, Inc., p. 5 dog and cat; © Ryan McVay/Photodisc Green/Getty Images, p. 14; © Shutterstock pp. 1 kitten, 6 cubes, paperclips, 7 hands, 10–11 kitten, measuring tape, ruler, 16–17 sofa, 18 pug puppy, 19 kitten lying down, 20–21, 22 Kit, 23 Jada and yarn, 24, 25, 29; © Stephen Dalton/Photo Researchers, Inc., pp.16–17; © SuperStock, Inc./Superstock, pp. 3, 31; © Warren Photographics, pp. 4, 12–13.

Cover photo: © Warren Photographics

Enslow Elementary
an imprint of
Enslow Publishers, Inc.
40 Industrial Road
Box 398
Berkeley Heights, NJ 07922
USA
http://www.enslow.com